We Sing Your Praise, O Lord

Dramas on Six Favorite Hymns

W. A. POOVEY

AUGSBURG Publishing House • Minneapolis

WE SING YOUR PRAISE, O LORD

These dramas also appear in *We Sing Your Praise, O Lord: Dramas and Meditations on Six Favorite Hymns*, which also contains six meditations that may be used in conjunction with the dramas. Each play, however, does present a complete message. It can be presented alone or followed by a discussion period. No performance fee is required if a copy of the play is purchased for each player.

Contents

The Expert

Characters

Jɪᴍ—Middle-aged, plumber, a man of faith.

Gᴇᴏʀɢᴇ—Same age. An English Professor. Skeptical but troubled.

Setting

Living room at George's home. Only two chairs needed but other furniture may be added to give appearance of a well-to-do household.

Costumes

Jɪᴍ wears working clothes. Gᴇᴏʀɢᴇ is dressed simply but his clothing indicates he is well-to-do.

(As the scene opens, George *is seated in one of the chairs, reading. He stands as* Jim *enters, carrying his plumbing tools in a case.)*

Jim: Well, George, I don't think that faucet will give you any more trouble for a while.

George: Say, that was quick. Didn't take you long.

Jim: It doesn't take a licensed plumber very long to put a new washer in a leaky faucet.

George: A new washer! I changed the washer in that faucet last week. And it didn't help a bit.

Jim: So you're the one. I noticed somebody had been fooling around, making some do-it-yourself repairs. *(Laughs.)* You put the wrong sized washer in it, George. And then you forgot to tighten the faucet again. No wonder it kept on leaking.

George: Wouldn't you know! I'm about as much use around a house as a bumblebee. It doesn't make sense. You just went to high school, Jim. I went on to college and graduate school and finished with a Ph.D. in English literature. And yet you fix a faucet in five minutes that baffled me even after I worked two hours on the blasted thing. Guess education doesn't pay.

Jim: Don't be silly. I'm a plumber. You're an English professor. I couldn't give a five-minute talk on Chaucer or Shakespeare if my life depended on it. Everybody's an expert at something. And we're all ignorant about a lot of things.

George: *(Laughs.)* Guess you're right. Say, it was a real surprise when I called the plumbing company today and then you walked in the door. Didn't expect to see you after all these years. You know, we were such good pals in high school but somehow we drifted away from each other.

JIM: *(Dryly.)* We've been moving in different circles, George. I haven't been invited to have tea at the university where you teach for a long time. But I'll have to admit my showing up here today wasn't a coincidence. When I saw your name on that work order, I volunteered for the job. Guess I wanted to see how my old classmate was doing.

GEORGE: I'm glad you came. Say, why don't you sit down and chat for a while? I'm all alone in the house right now. We can do some reminiscing. That is, if you've got the time—and won't charge me twenty dollars an hour just to sit and talk.

JIM: Don't worry. Plumbers don't charge for talk. Just for back talk. I do have a little time. This is my last call for the day.

GEORGE: Good. Sit down then and tell me how life's been treating you for the past umpteen years. *(Indicates a chair.)*

JIM: Thanks. *(They both sit.)* The Lord's been good to me over the years, George.

GEORGE: *(Catching the stress.)* The Lord, eh. Got a family?

JIM: Oh, yes. I married Nelly Gorman a year after we graduated from high school. You remember her. She was in our class. Kind of a chunky blond. She's even a little more chunky now, but I love every pound of her. We've got a nice home over on the west side. And we've got three children, two girls and a boy.

GEORGE: Two girls and a boy. Sounds good. Everybody well and happy?

JIM: Oh, yes. Just fine. Kids are all in school yet. Hope to send them to college—if I can find enough leaky faucets to fix. But how about you? Looks like you're doing pretty well for yourself, judging by this house.

GEORGE: I can't complain. Getting all that education was a bit of a struggle. But I'm head of the English department at the university now and I do a bit of writing on the side. It all adds up to a tidy sum.

JIM: You always were the bright one. Straight A student. Valedictorian of the class. Unanimously voted most likely to succeed.

GEORGE: *(Pleased.)* You do remember, don't you. That all seemed terribly important to me when I was in high school. I suppose I would sneer at it now.

JIM: But what about your family? I thought I noticed some pictures in one of the rooms.

GEORGE: Oh, yes, I've got a family. Or at least I think have.

JIM: You think you have a family! What kind of statement is that?

GEORGE: Well—it's hard for me to admit it but since we're exchanging confidences—we've got two boys but one of them has run away from home twice in the last year and the other one threatens to do the same thing about once a week.

JIM: That's tough.

GEORGE: Yes. I don't know what gets into kids now. I suspect my two have gotten mixed up with drugs like so many young people these days.

JIM: You sure have my sympathy. That's a miserable business. Hard on your wife, too, I'm sure.

GEORGE: I guess it is. But Marta and I have been talking lately about getting a divorce and that's pushed the boys' problems into the background. That's why I said I didn't know whether I had a family or not. I'm really not sure where I stand from one day to the next.

JIM: I'm sorry, George.

GEORGE: So am I. Somehow things haven't worked out the way I planned them. I guess life seldom does. *(Pause.)* But let's not talk about my troubles. I didn't mean to bring them into the conversation. I'd rather reminisce. Do you ever see any of the gang we both knew in high school?

JIM: Sometimes. I bumped into Eddie Johnson the other day. He's gained fifty pounds since we knew him. But wait a minute, George. I don't like the sound of things here. Aren't you doing something about your family troubles? Are you just letting your boys go? Are you and Marta just drifting into divorce?

GEORGE: I'm not sure it's any of your business but I have tried practically everything. Had the boys worked on by the school counselor and a professional psychiatrist. Didn't change a thing. And Marta and I have been to several marriage guidance clinics. Those experiences kept us from each other's throats for a while but nothing seems to help permanently. I guess it's just one of those things.

JIM: Have you talked over your problems with your pastor?

GEORGE: *(Stiffly.)* We don't have a pastor.

JIM: You don't! You used to go to church when I knew you. We all belonged to the same young people's group at St. Luke's.

George: I know. But you outgrow that stuff when you go to college. Religion and education just don't go together.

Jim: *(Bristling.)* You mean Christianity is just for dopes like me. People who never went beyond high school.

George: *(Conciliating.)* I didn't mean it that way, Jim. But you know, you get to studying and you find the Bible is full of old-fashioned ideas about sex and honesty and life in general. And you read all the idealistic stuff and all the myths and legends in that old book. And suddenly, bang, there goes your faith. It happens all the time.

Jim: My faith never went bang. I've gotten a lot of help and comfort from my church.

George: Such as—

Jim: Well, we've had some sickness and some trouble at times. I was even out of work for six months, recovering from an injury. And I don't think we would have made it if we hadn't had the promises of God to give us strength and pull us through.

George: *(Sneering.)* Oh, I know religion is a nice crutch to lean on. And I suppose you can't be blamed for believing the stuff they hand out in Sunday school and church if it makes you feel better. It's like my kids and the dope. It takes away all pain for a while.

Jim: *(Angry.)* Christianity isn't dope, George. It's strength and guidance for living.

George: Look, Jim, I don't want to quarrel with you. You weren't the brightest boy in our class and maybe you aren't any smarter now, even though you can fix a dripping faucet. If it makes you feel better to believe all that stuff about Jesus Christ and the importance of being good and going to heaven, OK. That's your business. I just don't buy it, that's all. *(Walks away.)*

JIM: *(After him.)* Did you ever think there might be some connection between your lack of faith in God and the trouble you're having with your boys and the disagreements between you and your wife?

GEORGE: Aw, come on. Now you're going to tell me that since you're a Christian, everything goes perfectly with you and your family.

JIM: I'm not going to tell you that because it would be a lie. Every member of my family, including yours truly, is an imperfect human being and becoming a Christian didn't change that. We make mistakes. We're thoughtless at times and we hurt one another. But we know we have a Savior who forgives us and we've learned to forgive one another. We've got love, and that makes the difference. And before I say something I'll be sorry for, I think I'd better be going. *(Picks up tools.)*

GEORGE: *(Coldly.)* Just as you say. I guess we don't see things eye to eye any more.

JIM: No! And my eyes are right where they've always been. Good luck, and God help you, George. *(Offers hand.)*

GEORGE: Yes, good luck and—God help me. *(Grabs JIM's hand and pulls him back to center stage.)* Jim, that did it. If you know any help, I sure could use it. I'm at the end of my rope.

JIM: I'm sorry. I shouldn't have argued with you. I should have recognized you were in deep trouble and depression.

GEORGE: I've been doing everything to keep my failures inside me. But I can't do it anymore. Jim, can you fix anything else than a leaky faucet—like a crushed ego or a broken heart?

JIM: Maybe God's hand guided me here today. What's the real trouble, George?

GEORGE: *(Sinking into chair and burying his head in hands.)* I don't know. I just don't know. But the past ten or fifteen years have been a literal hell for me and everybody in this household.

JIM: Strange. You seem to have everything here a man would want. You've got your education. You have a nice home and a wife and two boys. A lot of people would settle for that.

GEORGE: I thought I would settle for it too. These are the goals I had in mind even when I knew you in high school. But all this stuff doesn't mean anything when there's no love, no peace, no joy in a family. *(Pause.)* You sound like you've got a nice place to come home to after a day's work.

JIM: That's right. I'm always happy when the time comes to knock off plumbing and go spend some time with my family.

GEORGE: I can't tell you how many times I've stayed at the university and worked, just so I didn't have to come home until late at night. I'm only here today because everyone else is out and I can be alone. Jim, there's been quarreling and fighting almost every day in this house. No one wants to fight. We're all weary of battling each other. But it happens. The boys get at each other's throats and then Marta and I start in. We usually take opposite sides no matter what the question is. I suppose if she agreed with me I'd switch sides just to spite her.

JIM: Life's not meant to be lived like that, George.

GEORGE: I know. And we all make resolutions that we're not going to fight anymore, and the next day it starts up again. Look, Jim, do you really think it would do any good if we all went to church every Sunday. I'm willing to do anything to get a little peace and quiet here at home.

JIM: I don't think that would make any change, George. You'd be the same people when you came out of church you were when you went in.

GEORGE: In other words, it's hopeless. Too late for us. I should have kept on going to church when I was young but now religion won't do me any good.

JIM: Don't be silly, George. I'm not saying anything of the kind. But the answer to your problems isn't just go to church. Lots of people do that and aren't any happier than you are. The solution is to put yourself in the hands of an expert.

GEORGE: What do you mean, an expert?

JIM: Well, now look. You tried to fix that dripping faucet and you made a mess of it. Plumbing's not your business so you had to call in an expert. That's me. Plumbing is *my* business and I had the faucet fixed in five minutes. Catch on?

GEORGE: I'm with you so far.

JIM: All right. Now you've got another problem, a far worse one than a dripping faucet. You need an expert to show you how to live. And that's Jesus Christ. He said he was the way, the truth, and the life. He said he came into this world to bring us more abundant life. So, anybody who's having trouble finding an answer to life's problems needs to go to him. To the expert.

GEORGE: I see. You mean Jesus has a lot of rules to teach me. Some thou shalts and thou shalt nots. And if I follow the rules, everything will be fine. But we've tried rules and regulations. We've even written out contracts and agreed to live by them. And none of those contracts lasted a week.

JIM: I'm not surprised at that. No, George, it isn't a matter of adopting a code of conduct. Jesus Christ wants to take over your life. He's the expert and he wants you to put everything in his hands. You've got to surrender to him. Look, last Sunday we sang an old favorite hymn at church. You probably remember it from your church-going days. It's "Jesus, Savior, Pilot Me."

GEORGE: *(Thinking.)* It seems like I recollect it dimly.

JIM: The words of that song may not be great poetry, not the kind you deal with in your English literature classes. But they say what I'm trying to tell you. Let me see. I think can remember the first verse. Yes, it goes like this. *(He may sing or recite it.)*

> Jesus, Savior, pilot me
> Over life's tempestuous sea;
> Unknown waves before me roll,
> Hiding rock and treach'rous shoal;
> Chart and compass come from thee.
> Jesus, Savior, pilot me.

That's what I mean. Jesus is the expert, the pilot. "Chart and compass come from thee."

GEORGE: And you're saying this will solve all my troubles? All I have to do is put Jesus Christ in charge of things? That'll bring me peace and contentment?

JIM: I'm making no such promises. The hymn talks about waves and rocks and treacherous shoals. I'm just saying you'll never find any answer to living until you put your life in his hands.

GEORGE: What about my doubts, my intellectual problems?

JIM: Do you think you're the only one with doubts? Everybody has them. But maybe it's time to begin doubting your doubts. Bring the whole mess to Jesus, your doubts, your quarrels, your troubles with your sons. Put all your worries in Jesus' lap. Tell him, "You're the expert; take charge of everything."

GEORGE: It seems too much to hope for. Sounds like a miracle.

JIM: And you don't believe in miracles. I suppose that's some of your trouble with the Bible. I don't want to argue with you about such matters. But for once, believe in a miracle right here and now.

GEORGE: Jim, you're giving me hope. Maybe, just maybe things can change.

JIM: I tell you, they can. With Jesus as the expert pilot you'll steer a straight course. I know it. I know what he's done for me.

GEORGE: Will you come and talk to me again about this?

JIM: Of course. I don't want to push in where I'm not wanted. But would it help if Nelly and I and the family came over to see your family some night? We could talk about old times and perhaps about some new times for you.

GEORGE: Will you do that? Will you really come? Soon?

JIM: Sure. We'll come some evening after work. We can have a nice long talk. And I won't charge you time and a half for overtime.

In or Out?

Characters

Miss Elsa Peabody—Teacher, chairman of committee. Refined person.

Joseph McCall—Lawyer, rather loud and pugnacious.

Mrs. Molly McCall—Joseph's wife, rather shy.

Rev. Paul Johnson—Clergyman, a bit pompous at times.

Mrs. Betty Schmidt—Professional singer, sharp tongued, a sense of humor.

Setting

Five chairs are all that is required. A long table might be useful or a small one for the chairman. Committee members should face the audience.

Costumes

The usual dress-up costumes for people attending an important committee meeting.

(As the scene opens, all the cast are busy talking to one another. Finally Miss Peabody *takes her place at stage right and pounds on the desk to attract attention. Everyone quiets down.)*

Peabody: Ladies and gentlemen, it's time to begin our meeting. Please take your seats. *(Everyone sits down, facing the audience.* Molly *takes a chair at stage left.)*

McCall: Before we start our discussion, I have a favor to ask of the committee.

Peabody: What is it, Mr. McCall?

McCall: I think you've all met my wife, Molly. *(They look toward her. She smiles.)* She came along with me this time because we hope to do some shopping before we fly home tomorrow. I'm wondering if it will be all right if Molly sits here in the corner and reads a book while we meet. It seems better for her to be here than waiting around in a hotel room or admiring the rubber plants in the lobby.

Peabody: I'm sure we won't mind. Our deliberations aren't that secret. Does anybody object to Mrs. McCall's presence here today? *(All shake their heads and say, "No." "It's all right with me," etc.)*

Molly: Thank you very much.

Schmidt: I think Joseph McCall is just being smart. He doesn't want Molly to go shopping without him.

McCall: I can't pull anything over on Betty Schmidt.

Johnson: Perhaps Mrs. McCall can help us in our deliberations about the new hymnal we're planning.

Molly: No thank you, Rev. Johnson. My husband is the authority on church hymns in this family. I don't know anything about them except I know what I like.

SCHMIDT: That might be a real help to us. At times I'm not sure this committee knows *that* much about hymns.

MOLLY: If you don't mind, I'll just sit here in the corner and read my book. Then when the new hymnal is published, I can write and complain that you omitted all my favorites and included a lot of strange unsingable songs in the new publication.

PEABODY: You'll probably have to stand in line to register that complaint. Well, let's get down to business and let Mrs. McCall read her book. As you all know, the publishing company is anxious for us to complete our work. We're holding up the whole project of printing a new book of worship for our denomination. You must remember that we have approved fifty new hymns for inclusion in the hymnal and that means some old ones will have to go. We must keep the book down to a reasonable size. I hope we can finish our deliberations today, although we mustn't rush through our work. People are very touchy about hymns as Molly has reminded us, and although she was only teasing, I know we'll get a lot of nasty letters when the book is printed. So we want to be careful what we do.

SCHMIDT: All nasty letters should be referred immediately to the chairman.

PEABODY: I'm sure I'll get copies of critical letters, whether you send them to me or not. But now to business. At our last meeting we left off at number 309. So our next hymn to consider is 310, "Take my life and let it be Consecrated, Lord to thee." (*Some hymnals have "Take my life that I may be, Consecrated, Lord to thee." Use the version you are familiar with.)* As usual the question is: In or out? Do we keep this hymn or drop it to make way for some new songs? What's your pleasure?

JOHNSON: I don't see how you can omit this one. It's a great favorite in many churches.

SCHMIDT: It certainly is. I've sung it and heard it sung almost all my life. And that's a long time, believe me.

PEABODY: I think we used it last Sunday at my home church. The words were written, as you will note, by Frances Havergal, a famous writer of the last century. Well, we seem to be in accord on this one. But we haven't heard from you, Mr. McCall.

McCALL: You're going to hear now. I waited until you had all had your say, although I was sure how you would feel about number 310. *(Orating.)* Fellow committee members, I am unalterably opposed to including "Take my life and let it be Consecrated, Lord to thee," in our new publication.

SCHMIDT: My, you sound almost vengeful, McCall. This is a favorite hymn of thousands of people.

McCALL: I don't care if a million people choose it as number one on their hit parade. I think the hymn is a bad one and ought to be put to sleep for good. Our verdict on it should be: Out, not in!

PEABODY: Well, I didn't expect this. Is it the music you object to, Mr. McCall? I'll admit it isn't Bach or Beethoven.

McCALL: I don't care who wrote the music. It's the words that rile me. Anybody who sings this song is a hypocrite and I object to announcing publicly that I'm going to do a lot of things I don't have any intention of doing.

JOHNSON: I'm afraid I don't follow you, Mr. McCall. Can you be more specific in your charges?

McCALL: I intend to get specific, very specific. I expected the reaction everyone here has expressed, so I came prepared. (*Takes paper out of briefcase.*)

SCHMIDT: My stars, he's going to draw up an indictment against all of us.

McCALL: You're not far from the truth, Betty Schmidt. You all know I'm a lawyer and I'm not used to operating outside a courtroom. So if you don't mind I'll do a little examining today in the same manner as I would before a judge. I'd like to put the members of this committee on trial so I can prove my point about the hymn.

PEABODY: This is all very strange, but since you feel so strongly about it, the floor's yours, Mr. McCall.

SCHMIDT: (*Sarcastically.*) Do you want to put us all under oath so you can charge us with perjury if we don't tell the truth?

McCALL: That won't be necessary. But I'd like to begin with our chairman, Miss Peabody. (*He walks back and forth like a trial lawyer.*)

PEABODY: All right. I'm ready to be questioned—I think.

McCALL: Tell me, Miss Peabody, do you belong to any organizations that aren't exclusively religious?

PEABODY: Yes, I do. Since I'm a teacher, I have to belong to the PTA. I'm a member of the American Association of University Women. And I still attend meetings of my school sorority. Oh, yes, I belong to the Tuesday evening musical society and a bridge club.

McCALL: And do you do some work in these groups?

PEABODY: I do my share.

McCALL: Interesting. Now Miss Peabody, tell me how you can sing "Take my moments and my days; Let them flow in ceaseless praise"? It seems to me that a few of your moments don't fit into that pattern. Let me also read to you the second verse of this hymn:

> Take my hands and let them move
> At the impulse of thy love;
> Take my feet and let them be
> Swift and beautiful for thee.

Does that describe your daily life?

PEABODY: Not every day, I guess. But look here, Mr. McCall, I don't think the hymn demands that I do nothing but think about religion all day. And even if that's the meaning, you'll have to remember that none of us is perfect. I enjoy some of those other activities.

McCALL: I don't want to argue the point. I'm just stating my case against the hymn. Now I want to talk to Mrs. Betty Schmidt.

SCHMIDT: Oh, guilty as charged.

McCALL: Not so fast. We'll prove your guilt in a minute. You still do a lot of singing, don't you, Mrs. Schmidt?

SCHMIDT: Yes. The Lord has blessed me with a fair voice and I use it. And I sing in the church choir every Sunday, if that's what you want to know.

McCALL: I'm sure you help beautify the service. Your interest in music accounts for your presence on this committee and we are all in your debt. But you are also a member of the Gilbert and Sullivan society in your city. Isn't that right?

SCHMIDT: That's correct. I really love those operettas. I used to sing all the lovely female leads. Last year I sang Katisha, the old hag in *The Mikado*. Oh, well, that's the way it goes in this world.

McCall: None of us is getting any younger, Betty. I'm sure you don't regard Gilbert and Sullivan as religious music. But if that's so, how do you dare sing these words *(Reads from hymn)*:

> Take my voice and let me sing
> *Always, only,* for my king.

Schmidt: Why I—I—

McCall: Please note what comes next:

> Take my lips and let them be
> Filled with messages from thee.

Schmidt: Are you saying I'm doing wrong when I sing Gilbert and Sullivan songs?

McCall: I'm not saying anything. I'm just telling you what the hymn says. And now, Rev. Johnson.

Johnson: *(Resignedly.)* I knew my turn was coming.

McCall: Tell me, Rev. Johnson. You serve a large congregation, don't you?

Johnson: *(Proudly.)* Over a thousand members and growing all the time.

McCall: Yes, you're one of our denomination's most successful preachers. Your church is situated in a rather wealthy area, isn't it.

Johnson: I suppose I have one of the wealthiest congregations in our denomination. Or in any denomination, as a matter of fact.

McCall: Fine, fine. Are your members liberal contributors to the church?

JOHNSON: Yes, sir. We have an excellent stewardship record and our budget has increased by 25% in the past two years.

McCALL: It all sounds very good. Tell me, do any of your members go out to dinner at fancy restaurants after church services?

JOHNSON: I'm sure many of them do. Sometimes they even invite my wife and me to go along with them.

McCALL: How interesting. (*Springing the trap.*) Now let me read the first part of verse four of the hymn under discussion:

> Take my silver and my gold,
> Not a mite would I withhold.

Seems strange that your members would have any money left after they'd been to church on Sunday. That is, if they meant those words.

JOHNSON: Well—I—I—You know, McCall, I have thought of that at times. Wanted to take up the offering just after we sang those words.

McCALL: Ah, you catch on. But I'm not through with you yet, Rev. Johnson. The next line of the hymn says

> Take my intellect and use
> Every pow'r as thou shalt choose.

You're a man who works with his mind. Does all your intellect go for the Lord's work?

JOHNSON: I'm a sinful man, McCall. I do the best I can, but I do fall short.

SCHMIDT: I think this is cruel, Joseph McCall. You're treating us like you expect us to be angels, not human beings.

McCALL: I'm doing nothing of the kind. The hymn indicts all of us. Listen to the next verse:

Take my will and make it thine;
It shall be no longer mine.
Take my heart, it is thine own;
It shall be thy royal throne.

I wish I could measure up to that but I can't. And neither can anyone here. The demands of this hymn make hypocrites of all of us and I don't think it should be in our hymnal. Maybe Frances Havergal could live like that. Maybe Saint Francis of Assisi and the Apostle Paul could live like that. All right, let them sing the hymn. But I just don't think we have any right to include such impossibly pious sentiments in a church hymnal, because we can't measure up to them. And with that, I rest my case. *(Sits down. An awkward pause.)*

PEABODY: There's a lot in what you're saying, Mr. McCall. Maybe we ought to drop that one out of our book of worship. But I can just see the angry letters we'll get because of this.

JOHNSON: I'm not a lawyer and I can't make any rebuttal. But I'll be sorry if I have to vote to drop "Take my life and let it be Consecrated, Lord to thee" out of the hymnal.

PEABODY: But you do agree that Mr. McCall is right in his opposition?

JOHNSON: Reluctantly, reluctantly.

PEABODY: Are you changing your vote too, Betty?

SCHMIDT: I'm thinking. *(Pause.)* No, I don't agree. And I think I can prove that McCall is wrong.

JOHNSON: If you only can.

McCALL: *(Smugly.)* You're welcome to try.

SCHMIDT: But I will need the help of Mrs. McCall.

MOLLY: Me?

SCHMIDT: That's right.

MOLLY: But I told you I don't know anything about hymns.

SCHMIDT: I don't want your opinion about hymns. I want to know some things about Joseph McCall.

MOLLY: Oh, I don't think I ought to get mixed up in this at all.

SCHMIDT: Joseph McCall, how do you lawyers go about getting a reluctant witness to testify?

McCALL: Well, this isn't the way. But Molly, come on and take part here for a few minutes. *(She shakes her head.)* I'll buy you that watch you've been talking about if you help out here.

MOLLY: Well—if you put it that way. . . . *(MOLLY moves closer.)*

SCHMIDT: Thank you. Gross bribery of the witness. But we'll not let that get out of this room. Now tell me, Molly, how long have you and Joseph been married?

MOLLY: Thirty years. *(Adjust to age of couple.)*

McCALL: Is it that long?

MOLLY: Yes, and you'd better remember it when our anniversary comes around.

SCHMIDT: You've been warned. Tell me, Molly, do you think your husband loves you?

MOLLY: I'm sure of it.

SCHMIDT: Even though he's not with you every minute of the day?

MOLLY: I don't expect that.

SCHMIDT: Has he ever told you that he loves you?

MOLLY: Yes. He's not a shy man in such things.

SCHMIDT: Good, good. Now let me ask you. Did your husband ever do anything to displease you since you've been married?

McCALL: Here, what kind of questioning is this?

SCHMIDT: You asked some pretty personal questions of us, Joseph McCall. Tell me, Molly, did your husband ever do anything to upset you or make you wish he hadn't done it?

MOLLY: Well—yes. He's not perfect, you know. I can remember how we fought over the way he squeezed a toothpaste tube—

McCALL: Oh, Molly, for goodness sake—

MOLLY: Well, we did argue over it until we got the bright idea of buying two tubes and each squeezing our own tube the way we wanted to do it. And sometimes Joseph came home late from the office and forgot to call me and my dinner was spoiled.

SCHMIDT: But you didn't doubt that he loved you, despite these slips, did you?

MOLLY: Oh, no. You see, love was the goal we had for each other. We didn't always reach the goal, but we tried. And year after year we've come closer to each other.

SCHMIDT: Thank you. I couldn't have put it better. I don't have any more questions because you've made the point I wanted to stress about the hymn.

JOHNSON: I think I'm beginning to see the light.

McCall: I'm afraid I am too.

Schmidt: It's very simple. I don't think this hymn is saying we're perfect or likely to become so. It sets a goal for us. Mr. McCall was busy quoting the verses to us but he left out the last one. Let me read it.

> Take my love; my Lord, I pour
> At thy feet its treasure store;
> Take myself, and I will be
> Ever, only, all for thee.

I think that's a beautiful ending to the hymn. It says exactly what I want my life to be. And I think we need this hymn to remind us of our goals, our dreams. Maybe singing the words makes Mr. McCall feel like a hypocrite but it doesn't affect me that way. It makes me go out of church resolved to let Christ come closer to me, resolved to let him fill my life more than he has in the past. "Take my life" pledges my love to my Lord the same way as Mr. McCall pledges his love to Molly, even though he falls short at times. I think we need this hymn as a love song to God. *(Sits down.)*

Peabody: I like that. A love song to God! *(They applaud.)*

McCall: Guess I'll have to join in the applause, too. You've been the better lawyer today, Betty Schmidt.

Schmidt: Oh, no, I'm just an old Gilbert and Sullivan singer. But someday I hope to sing in a great choir in heaven, if they'll have me. And I'll not sing off key there.

Peabody: I'm sure you'll get your wish, Betty. Right now I judge the verdict is: Number 310 is in. *(All nod their heads.)*

Only a Footnote

Characters

MOTHER—In late 40s.

BETTY—Girl about 22.

DORA—Fairly young.

PETER—An older man.

ZILPAH—About MOTHER's age.

LEAH—Younger woman, talkative.

PURNIA—Fairly young. *(Optional)*

AUGUSTINE—About Peter's age. *(Optional)*

ELSA—Fairly young. *(Optional)*

REV. LOEHE—Middle aged. *(Optional)*

JANE—Young college girl.

MARIE—Same age as JANE.

VOICE OFF STAGE

Note: The cast seems large but because of the brief scenes, the parts can be doubled and the number of actors reduced as desired.

Setting

The stage should be bare.

Costumes

Characters in the first and last scenes should wear contemporary clothing. Appropriate biblical costumes and other types of clothing can be used in the middle sketches. Since the characters are playing "what if" scenes, all characters in the middle scenes can wear robes or albs if desired.

(As the scene opens, Mother *and* Betty *stand facing each other, evidently in the midst of a bitter argument.)*

Mother: Now Betty, I don't want to hear another word about it. Your father and I had a long discussion last night. And for once we were in complete agreement. You will have to give up this whole idea of becoming a nurse on a mission station.

Betty: Mother, did it ever occur to you that I'm an adult and perfectly capable of making up my own mind and going into missionary work whether you and dad say I can or not?

Mother: *(Whining.)* Oh, of course, if you're anxious to break your mother's heart. And your father's too, if he'll admit it.

Betty: Don't say that! You know I don't want to break anybody's heart. Haven't I always been an obedient daughter?

Mother: *(Reluctantly.)* Up until now—yes, you have. But you've given us lots of worried nights since you started with this missionary idea.

Betty: Mother! I talked about being a missionary when I was only six years old.

Mother: I know. But nobody paid any attention to that. Little boys at six want to be firemen when they grow up. If they all did, we'd have to burn down half the town just to give them something to do. Childhood dreams are just that—dreams, things to be forgotten.

Betty: Mine wasn't a dream. I've never stopped thinking about going somewhere to help people. You know I always went to hear missionaries speak at the church when they returned on furlough. And I took courses in school that would be useful on a mission field. That's why I studied nursing.

MOTHER: *(Accusingly.)* You never told us that!

BETTY: No, because I didn't want to start this fight before it became necessary.

MOTHER: But Betty, why do you want to traipse off to India or Africa or some other godforsaken place to do mission work?

BETTY: Just because some of those places are godforsaken, or seem to be. Look, Mother, there are people in the world who haven't even heard about Jesus Christ. There are sick and starving children who need help and I think I can help them.

MOTHER: Can't you help somebody here at home? Me, for instance?

BETTY: I happen to feel God wants me to work among people who have never heard the gospel. And that's what I'm aiming to do.

MOTHER: I suppose Rev. Corwin is back of all this. He probably filled your ears with propaganda when you met with him last week.

BETTY: Sorry to disappoint you, but Rev. Corwin tried to talk me out of the whole idea.

MOTHER: Well! I find that hard to believe. He's a minister and he's supposed to be in favor of mission work.

BETTY: And you're a Christian and you should be in favor of mission work too. But Rev. Corwin wanted to be sure I was sincere in my goal. He tried all the arguments he could think of to get me to change my mind. When we finished talking, he was sure I meant what I said.

So he just told me, "God be with you," and let it go at that.

MOTHER: Is that all he said?

BETTY: No. He said I would have trouble with you and dad.

MOTHER: Oh, he did, did he!

BETTY: And how right he was. Look, Mother, why are you so opposed to my doing this? You've never been against mission work before. I've even heard you sing, "O Zion Haste, Your Mission High Fulfilling," as if you really meant it.

MOTHER: I'm not against mission work in general. I'm against your throwing your life away like this. I've always given to our church's collections for missions, even though your father has objected. He always says, "Those people have a religion. Leave them alone." I've never felt that way. But when it comes to my only daughter traveling to some wild place to nurse half-savage people, I draw the line.

BETTY: Mother, those people in other lands have bodies that need to be healed and souls that need to be saved. Christ died for them too.

MOTHER: I'm sure you know all the arguments in favor of your becoming a missionary nurse. But I'm not going to discuss the matter any more. If you love me and your dad, you'll stay home and get a job at St. Luke's Hospital. Then maybe you'll marry a nice young man and settle down and raise a family. That's my hope for you.

BETTY: (*Exasperated.*) Mother! You're so unfair and so wrong. Have you ever thought what would have happened if everyone in the past had thought the way you do? There wouldn't have been any missionaries to bring the gospel to our ancestors. We would be the heathen, living in what you call a godforsaken land. What if that had happened? What if—

BETTY *and* MOTHER *exit during this final speech. Then a voice comes over the loudspeaker or is heard offstage.)*

VOICE: What if—what if—what if—

(PETER *and* DORA *enter, from opposite sides, if possible.*

PETER *is carrying a bag of clothes.)*

DORA: Why Simon Peter, you look like you're all packed up and ready to leave Jerusalem.

PETER: That's right. I'm heading for my home in Galilee.

DORA: But Peter, I thought the Master told you to wait here in Jerusalem until you received the Holy Spirit.

PETER: *(Reluctantly.)* There was some talk about that.

DORA: And you're starting out to spread the good news without waiting for the Spirit? Do you think that's wise?

PETER: I don't happen to be going on a preaching trip, Dora. I'm going home to start up my fishing business again.

DORA: Your fishing business!

PETER: That's right. I was a fisherman once upon a time and I think I can still row a boat and throw a net into the water. At least I'm going to try again.

DORA: But I thought you were supposed to catch men. Didn't Jesus tell you to go make disciples everywhere, baptizing and teaching all the truth he taught?

PETER: That's right. I'll not deny he said it. But you can't hold me to that, Dora. Last night all eleven of us had a meeting and decided we weren't going to go chasing all over the world, telling people what they should believe or do. After all, even Jesus didn't have too much success preaching to people and he was the best preacher who ever lived. Why would anyone think eleven fishermen and tax collectors and what have you will do any better?

DORA: *(Sadly.)* So you don't believe the things he taught you! Even after seeing him alive since his crucifixion. You don't believe, any of you!

PETER: Of course we believe. We're all convinced Jesus is the Messiah and we'll try to follow the way he taught. It's just that we want to live sane, normal lives at home. My wife's been nagging me lately to spend more time with her and I'm going to do it. And James and John have to take care of their mother. Everybody's got something. We've all agreed that when we get a chance, we'll talk to people around us about Jesus. The good news will get around somehow.

DORA: I certainly hope so. But it doesn't seem likely to me. (PETER *and* DORA *exit. The voice is heard again.)*

VOICE: What if— What if— What if—

(ZILPAH *and* LEAH *appear. If they can enter from opposite sides of the stage and meet in the center, it will help.)*

ZILPAH: Oh, Leah, I'm glad to see you. I've got some wonderful news for you.

LEAH: *(Excitedly.)* What is it? Did your husband find a treasure in your backyard? Is your daughter going to marry a rich husband? Did your goat have twin kids?

ZILPAH: Not so fast. Nothing like that.

LEAH: Well, what is it? Tell me, tell me.

ZILPAH: I will, if you'll give me a chance. Remember that preacher we heard the other day? The one who told such good news about a man named Jesus?

LEAH: Oh, yes. His name was Saul—or Paul. They seemed to call him both names. He made such a fine speech. I could listen to him every day.

ZILPAH: You're going to get your chance to do just that.

LEAH: *(Laughs.)* Not likely. He's a traveling evangelist, Zilpah. He's been to all kinds of places.

ZILPAH: I know. I know. He's been to Lystra and Derbe and Damascus and Antioch and I don't know where else. But he's through traveling. He's going to settle down right here in Troas.

LEAH: How do you know that? It doesn't sound like something an evangelist would do. In Troas, yet.

ZILPAH: It's true, Leah. Paul's traveling companion, Silas, told my daughter Millah all about it this morning. They've become good friends this past week.

LEAH: I remember Silas. He didn't do much speaking the other day.

ZILPAH: He's been talking plenty since then. He told Millah all about Paul, about his conversion on the road to Damascus and about the strange things that have happened to him since then. But the strangest thing happened last night. You see, Paul was all set to start out tomorrow to preach his good news someplace else. And then while he was sleeping Paul had a vision.

LEAH: A vision? Right here in Troas?

ZILPAH: No reason why you can't have a vision here in Troas as well as anyplace else.

Leah: I suppose not. And the vision told Paul to stay here and work?

Zilpah: No, it didn't. The way Silas tells it, Paul saw a man from Macedonia who asked him to come over to that land and preach his message there too.

Leah: Over to Europe? Say, this is exciting. But you say Paul isn't going? Did he think the man in the vision was a demon, trying to lure him to a watery grave?

Zilpah: Oh, Leah, such an imagination. No, silly. But this vision made Paul think about what his life had been up until now. He's been traveling around for years, trying to help people. And he's had people arguing with him and threatening to put him in prison. He's had rocks thrown at him and other hateful things done to him. And now this—a call to go into a whole new area. Paul just decided he's had enough. He was tired of the whole business.

Leah: I would think he would be.

Zilpah: And that's why he decided to stay right here in Troas. Said there were plenty of sinners right here to preach to.

Leah: He's right about that. Why, let me tell you what I heard about old Esau and his servant—

Zilpah: I believe one of the sins Paul particularly wants to denounce here is gossip.

Leah: Oh, all right. I'll be quiet. But did Paul think it was right for him to stay here and not go to Macedonia? Maybe this Jesus will be angry at him for refusing to obey the vision.

Zilpah: I don't know about that. But Paul did tell Silas he

thought people in Macedonia were wild and uncivilized and wouldn't appreciate the good news anyway.

LEAH: That's right. Macedonians don't deserve any good news. But I'm glad Paul is going to stay here. He's a bachelor, isn't he? (ZILPAH *nods.*) Maybe we can find a wife for him here.

ZILPAH: Who knows? (*Exit* LEAH *and* ZILPAH. *The* VOICE *is heard again.*)

VOICE: What if— what if— what if— (*If more time is needed between scenes, the organist can play a verse from "O Zion, Haste," before each scene begins. If desired, one or both of the next scenes can be omitted.*)

PURNIA: (*Entering and confronting* AUGUSTINE *who has come from the other side of stage.*) It's not a ghost? It's really you, Augustine?

AUGUSTINE: In the flesh.

PURNIA: But I thought you had left for that island off the coast somewhere. You were supposed to go with forty monks to preach the good news to the natives there. Pope's orders and all that.

AUGUSTINE: I'm still here.

PURNIA: But what happened?

AUGUSTINE: Cold feet. Or the prospect of cold feet, at least. My dear Purnia, do you know anything about Britain, that island you mentioned?

PURNIA: Not much, except it's a long ways from Rome.

AUGUSTINE: A long *cold* way, my dear. Britain is a land of rain and fog and brr—snow! I've been reading about it and talking to people who've been there. And the reports don't sound good.

Purnia: But the pope was so definite about your going. And so interested. Didn't he see some of the inhabitants in the slave market?

Augustine: So it would seem. At least they're telling a romantic story of how Pope Gregory saw some blond boys for sale and asked who they were. When he was told they were Angles, from Anglo-Saxons, you know, he said they were Angels, not Angles. So the story goes.

Purnia: How touching!

Augustine: And how wrong. From what I've heard, *devils* would describe the people better than *angels*.

Purnia: But then they need the gospel badly. And you're defying the pope by staying here in Rome.

Augustine: My dear, Pope Gregory has lots of irons in the fire. All I need to do is drag my feet a little and he will forget all about this silly expedition. That way I'll be saved from some unpleasant experiences.

Purnia: And the people of Britain won't hear the gospel.

Augustine: Purnia, that far-off island will never amount to anything. It doesn't make any difference whether we convert them or not. Besides, there is plenty of work to do right here in Rome. I intend to stay here where the sun is warm and the food agrees with me. (Purnia *and* Augustine *exit and the* Voice *is heard again.*)

Voice: What if— what if— what if—

(Rev. Loehe *enters, reading a book.* Elsa *hurries after him.*)

Elsa: Rev. Loehe, Rev. Loehe. You have a letter from America. A sailor brought it to the parsonage just now. (*Hands* Loehe *the letter.*)

Loehe: Thank you, Elsa. (*Puts letter in pocket.*)

ELSA: I wonder what could be in the letter.

LOEHE: *(Smiling.)* I suppose the best way is to open it and see. *(Takes letter from pocket and looks at it.)* It's probably from my old friend August Schmidt who went to America last year. He promised to write and tell me about conditions there.

ELSA: I don't understand how anybody could think of traveling so far in a boat.

LOEHE: A great many of our people have gone to America in the past few years. *(He opens the letter.)* Ah, yes. The letter is from Mr. Schmidt. *(ELSA starts to leave.)* Wait a minute, Elsa, and I'll read the letter to you.

ELSA: Oh, thank you. I'm so interested. *(LOEHE reads letter aloud.)*

LOEHE: My dear Rev. Loehe. I have meant to write to you for some time but have been traveling around this big country and haven't gotten to my writing until now. I feel I must tell you of the needs here. *(Looks up.)* Sounds like he wants to borrow some money. No, I don't believe that's it. Rev. Loehe, you know a lot of our German people have moved to this new land in the past few years. They've scattered all over America. Unfortunately many of them are drifting away from their Lord. There aren't enough German-speaking clergy here and many of our people haven't learned English yet. So they don't go to church and their children receive no instructions in the Christian faith. Could you send us some workers? We need pastors and theological students. Please help or the church will die out among many of our people, and once dead, it will be hard to bring to life again. Signed, your friend in Christ, August Schmidt. *(Puts letter away.)* Well, Elsa, what do you think of that?

ELSA: Oh, I feel so sorry for those poor people, living in a strange land with no churches and no pastors.

LOEHE: I can understand your feelings, Elsa. But let me remind you that no one made those people go to America. It was their own choice.

ELSA: That's right. But America offered them so many opportunities. Free land, a chance to live in a new world where old customs wouldn't hold them back. A place to fulfill dreams.

LOEHE: That's the right word—dreams. The people who went off to America were dreamers, thinking life would be better someplace else. Now they find it isn't quite as pleasant as they thought. I feel sorry for them too.

ELSA: *(Eagerly.)* Then you're going to answer Mr. Schmidt's appeal? You're going to try to get some pastors and students to go to America?

LOEHE: Not so fast, Elsa. Sometimes people have to pay for their foolishness. I feel sorry for the Germans in America. But I would feel even sorrier for a pastor or student who would have to leave home and go to that wilderness land. I'm afraid I'll have to write to Mr. Schmidt and tell him we need all our pastors and theological students right here in Germany. (LOEHE *and* ELSA *exit.)*

VOICE: What if— what if— what if— *(If the play seems too long for presentation, it would be possible to cut one or more of the above scenes but the impact is greater if all can be presented.)*

(JANE *and* MARIE *enter from opposite sides and meet at stage center.)*

JANE: *(Listlessly.)* Hello, Marie. (JANE *carries an armful of books.)*

MARIE: Hello, Jane. You look like you just lost your last boy-friend. What's the matter?

JANE: Nothing. I just flunked a test in Comparative Religion, that's all.

MARIE: That's a shame. Didn't you study for it?

JANE: Of course I studied. I stayed up almost all night cramming for that exam. Then the prof asked a question I couldn't even start to answer. Marie, have you ever heard of a religious group known as Christians?

MARIE: No, I don't think so.

JANE: Neither have I, and that's why I flunked the test. Here, hold my books. I'm going to look up the answer right now. (MARIE *takes all the books except one.* JANE *looks in the index and then finds the article.*) Here it is. Page 62. Well, wouldn't you know! The answer is a footnote. I call that pretty rotten, asking a question about a foot-note.

MARIE: Old Prof Pardy is pretty tricky. What does the book say about this Christian group?

JANE: I'll read it. Christians—a religious group of the first century of the common era. The religion was centered in Palestine and believed in a certain Jesus who sup-posedly was crucified and then rose from the dead. Christians had high moral standards and might have developed into an important group. Unfortunately the followers of this Jesus weren't very energetic in spreading their religion and by the year 100, the Christian religion ceased to exist. (*Looks up.*) That's all it says.

MARIE: How stupid. You would think people would know better. If you have something worth believing, you've got to get out and spread the good news around. Otherwise you end up as nothing but a footnote.

JANE: Yes, and I end up with a failure in my course. *(Exit.)*

VOICE: What if— what if— what if? But thanks be to God, it didn't happen that way!

The Storm

Characters

Fred Jones—Middle-aged, slow talking, nervous at end of play.
Jane Jones—Fred's wife, sane and sensible but upset by storm.
Gladys Peterson—Friendly, sympathetic.
Mr. Harding—The town banker, matter of fact, not pompous.
Mary—Young girl, aged 9 to 12.

Setting

A ruined house after a tornado has passed through. Just some rubble is all that is necessary to suggest what has happened.

Costumes

Ordinary street clothes. Fred and Gladys can wear work clothes.

(As the scene opens, FRED *and* JANE *enter and stand looking at the wreckage of their home. They stand silently for a moment before* FRED *speaks.)*

FRED: Well, Jane, here we are again. The place looks just as big a mess as it did yesterday. It'll probably take several weeks before the city gets around to cleaning up the rubble along this street.

JANE: Oh, Fred, every time I look at what used to be our home, I could just cry my eyes out. *(Begins to poke into the rubble.)*

FRED: *(Dryly.)* You've already cried your eyes out on Monday, Tuesday, and Wednesday of this week. I thought you'd never stop. Tears won't bring back our home.

JANE: I know. I know.

FRED: There's really no point in our being here today. There's nothing we can do until all this rubbish is hauled away. *(Noticing her.)* What are you poking around in that mess for?

JANE: *(Stops.)* I keep thinking I might find a letter or a picture or something underneath this rubble.

FRED: Not much chance of that. All the light stuff blew away when the storm hit. Our papers and things will probably turn up someplace in the next county. That usually happens when a tornado hits an area.

JANE: I guess you're right. Everything is gone and that's what makes it so hard. I know we'll get another house somehow. But all my pretty things—my china and pictures and letters and all the keepsakes you've given me over the years—all gone. And you can't replace such things.

FRED: *(Dryly.)* We still have each other as keepsakes, you know.

JANE: I know. And everybody says we were lucky to come our of this storm alive. When I look at this pile of rubble, I wonder how we made it. But I keep thinking—why did it have to happen at all? Why weren't we *real* lucky, lucky enough to have the storm miss us completely? Why did we get hit and other people escape? And I can't find any answer to that.

FRED: When you come up with an answer, let me know. There never seems to be any rhyme or reason to a tornado.

JANE: I know. The wind hits so haphazardly. There's Mr. Jordan down the street that everybody says is neglecting his wife and carrying on with two married women. He comes home drunk almost every night and he never goes to church. And his home wasn't hit at all.

FRED: Would you feel better if he had been wiped out like we were?

JANE: Oh, I didn't mean it that way. But you know what I'm trying to say.

FRED: Yes, I know. All my prize roses were wiped out too. The back wall fell on all the bushes. And I thought I was going to have some real winners this year.

JANE: I'm sorry about your roses, Fred. You worked so hard with them. All this is going to make it difficult in church next Sunday. Everybody is going to pity us and tell us how sorry they are that our house was hit.

FRED: It's not going to be hard for me. I'm not going to church Sunday.

JANE: Now Fred, we always go to church on Sunday. And your blue suit you had on when the storm struck will be OK. And Mildred Johnson will lend me some clothes. We wear the same size in everything.

FRED: It's not a question of clothes. I'm not going to church next Sunday or any other Sunday.

JANE: Fred, don't be bitter. You've been so brave up until now. I guess I shouldn't have complained but I can't help it once in a while.

FRED: Your complaints had nothing to do with the way I feel. I simply refuse to go and worship a God who lets me down like this.

JANE: You mustn't blame God for this. I can't understand why it happened but I'm not blaming God.

FRED: Well, I am. Do you remember what happened in church last Sunday?

JANE: Not particularly. It was just like any other Sunday.

FRED: No it wasn't. They sang one of my favorite hymns—This Is My Father's World. And that song has destroyed all my faith in God.

JANE: We didn't sing that badly, Fred.

FRED: I don't mean that. Do you remember the words to that hymn?

JANE: You know I don't remember things like that.

FRED: Well, I do. It goes like this

> This is my Father's world,
> And to my list'ning ears
> All nature sings, and round me rings
> The music of the spheres.
> This is my Father's world;

> I rest me in the thought
> Of rocks and trees, of skies and seas;
> His hand the wonders wrought.

JANE: So—

FRED: It's very simple. If God gets credit for the rocks and trees, he has to take the blame for the tornadoes and earthquakes too. The song says God shines in all that's fair. Well, he didn't shine very brightly when he let that terrible wind blow through here. Dozens of houses hit and lots of people injured. Three people killed. I tell you I'll never have any confidence again in a God who lets things like that happen.

JANE: Oh, Fred, you mustn't talk like that.

FRED: Why not? I'm just saying what other people feel about this whole mess.

JANE: I do wish you would go and talk to the pastor about all this.

FRED: Oh, sure. And he'll just say *(mockingly)*, Trust in the Lord. All things work together for good. *(Normal voice.)* And more of the same. I'm not buying that line.

JANE: *(Looking off in distance.)* Well, for goodness sake, keep your opinions to yourself. We'll talk this out later. Here comes Gladys Peterson and she's a good friend of ours and a member of our church. You don't want her to hear you saying such things. It'll upset her.

FRED: I'm not going to upset anybody. This is between God and me.

JANE: Hello, Gladys.

GLADYS: Hello, Jane. *(They embrace.)* My, I'm so sorry. Hello, Fred.

Fred: Hello, Gladys. *(They shake hands.)*

Gladys: *(Looks at wreckage.)* My, my, it's worse than I thought. Just makes a person want to cry, to see all this mess.

Fred: Jane has done plenty of crying the past three days. Enough to flood the whole town, I think, so you needn't bother, Gladys.

Jane: He feels just as badly as I do. But men aren't supposed to cry. Poor creatures. I pity them.

Gladys: It's just a shame to think what the storm did to you. But I didn't come down here to commiserate with you. I've come with what I hope is good news.

Fred: We could use a little of that right now.

Gladys: I'm sure you know the people in the church are all upset about your losses. Our prayer chain has been busy every day remembering you in our prayers. But we haven't just been praying. We've been busy making a few plans to help you. And I think we can ease things for you a little bit.

Fred: We don't want any charity. This has been a bad loss but we'll make out all right, thank you just the same.

Jane: Fred! Let Gladys tell us what she has in mind.

Fred: All right. But we're not charity patients yet.

Gladys: If someone else were in trouble, I know you people would help them. And we want to help you now. I hear you've been living at the Starlight Motel since Sunday night and I'm sure you don't want to stay there until you can get your house built again.

Fred: Probably couldn't afford it.

GLADYS: I don't suppose many of us could. So our friendship committee at the church has found a nice home for you to live in. It's over on Chestnut Street, near here and the rent is low. The people who lived there just moved out, so the place is empty and you can move in tomorrow if you want to.

JANE: But Gladys, we haven't got anything to move in. We didn't save any of our furniture or clothing. We'll have to start all over and buy everything new. And I don't see how we can afford to do that—not until we get our insurance money anyway.

FRED: At least we've got two chairs and a bed at the motel.

GLADYS: Nobody expects you to move into an empty house. We've canvassed the church members and we have enough furniture promised to take care of all your needs.

JANE: That's very kind.

FRED: Yes. I suppose everybody has some cast-off things in a storeroom they can lend us.

GLADYS: No, no. No cast-offs. You see, we all realized how fortunate we were not to get hit by that tornado. And we said, right from the start, that you weren't going to get beat-up chairs and tables to begin living again. So everybody has donated something from their own homes and has agreed not to replace it until you're settled in your own home again. A missing davenport or table or stove will be a reminder of how blessed we have been to have escaped the storm.

FRED: Yes, while we took the brunt of it. Any idea why we got the blow and you other people escaped?

GLADYS: Fred, I've turned that over and over in my mind.

You've always been good church members, better than most of the rest of us. I simply can't understand why you got hit and the rest of us escaped.

FRED: I don't know either. But I can tell you one thing. I'm through being a good church member.

JANE: Fred! You said you wouldn't talk like that in front of Gladys.

FRED: I'm sorry, but she might as well know the truth. I think God played a dirty trick on us when he let that storm strike our house. There's no way I can get even with him. A man can't fight God. But I'm not going to go on acting like I'm a Christian when everything I've got is lying buried in that pile of rubble.

GLADYS: Fred, I can sympathize with you. But being bitter won't help.

FRED: I'm not being bitter. Just honest.

JANE: But think of the nice things the church people are going to do for us. Finding us a house and lending us their furniture. Doesn't that say something to you about the church and about God?

FRED: I appreciate what Gladys and the others are offering. It does them proud, but they're just being kind to people in trouble. And you don't have to be religious to do a thing like that.

GLADYS: No, but it helps. If God was good enough to give us his son, it's not asking much for us to help one another.

FRED: I don't want to argue. I'm just seeing the world through different eyes.

JANE: Look, here comes Mr. Harding, our friend at the bank.

FRED: I suppose he's come to collect our next house payment.

GLADYS: You are bitter, Fred. Don't let this thing destroy you.

HARDING: *(Appearing and shaking hands as he talks.)* Hello, Fred and Jane. I thought I'd find you here. And Mrs. Peterson. How are you?

GLADYS: Just fine.

FRED: Hello, Harding. Quite a mess, isn't it?

HARDING: It certainly is. I drove by here last night and saw all this for the first time. Nothing left, I'm afraid.

FRED: No. I suppose I'm going to be paying you house payments on a pile of junk.

HARDING: I think your insurance will cover the rest of your debt, Fred. But you'll not have enough left to cover the cost of a new home.

FRED: Are you here to offer me a new loan? At 15%, perhaps?

HARDING: Fred, you know you can get a government disaster loan for less interest than that. No, I'm here with some very special news.

JANE: We can use all the good news available right now. Gladys brought us some already.

FRED: If we decide to take up her offer.

HARDING: Well, I have an offer that I think you won't turn down. Yesterday afternoon a man who insists on remaining anonymous came into the bank and said he was concerned about your loss. He told me to offer you whatever you need to rebuild your home, at no rate of interest. And you can take your time in paying off the loan.

JANE: Oh, how wonderful.

GLADYS: My, that makes my news seem rather small.

FRED: But I don't understand. Why would anybody do a thing like that? I don't know anybody who's got that kind of money.

HARDING: You're not supposed to know him. But he knows you. He said he was always impressed by the fact you were a good faithful couple, always in church on Sundays, always willing to help out other people. He thought it was too bad that someone like you should have to suffer such a terrible loss. So he was moved to make this offer.

JANE: Isn't that wonderful!

GLADYS: I guess it's at a time like this that people really show the goodness of their hearts.

JANE: Now, aren't you sorry you said so many bitter things, Fred?

FRED: No, I'm not. The preacher always said when people desert you, God helps you. But this is just the opposite. God deserted me and people are just trying to undo the evil God caused.

HARDING: Fred, we don't know why these things happen.

FRED: No we don't. But they certainly don't happen to show us how much God loves us. Mr. Harding, your anonymous friend has made us a wonderful offer. And you've been very kind too, Gladys. But if all this depends on our being good church members, I'm going to have to refuse your help, because I'm not going to be a good church member any more. I'm not going to be a hypocrite and sing about this being God's world and how he shines in all that's fair. Not after an experience like this.

HARDING: I can understand how you feel.

GLADYS: Fred, we're helping you because we love you and you need our help. We're not trying to reward you for church attendance and we're not asking you what you're going to do from now on.

HARDING: I think the same goes for your anonymous friend. With that understanding, you will take the help, won't you?

FRED: *(Breaking down.)* I don't know. I don't know. I've got to think this all out. So much has happened. I can still hear that storm raging and I can see the walls of the house caving in. I watched everything we owned blow away. You people will have to give me time to think. I'm all confused about God and goodness and love and the whole business. I just don't know what to think or say. *(Buries his face in his hands and turns his back on the audience.)*

GLADYS: He *can* cry. It'll do him good.

JANE: I wish I could help him. It's the shock of all this.

MARY: *(From offstage.)* Mr. Jones. Mr. Jones. *(Enters.)* I've got something for you. *(Keeps the rose hidden, behind her back.)*

GLADYS: It's the little girl from down the street.

JANE: How are you, Mary?

MARY: I'm all right. And I'm sorry about your house.

HARDING: We're all sorry, my dear.

MARY: I've got something for Mr. Jones.

FRED: *(Turning around.)* I'm sorry I broke down like this. I'm just tired, I guess. Oh, hello, Mary. What have you got for me?

MARY: Well, mother told me I shouldn't play around your house since it all blew down, because I might step on a nail or bang my knee. But I did look around in the back and there was one place where a board fell across one of your rose bushes.

FRED: Boards fell on all my rose bushes, Mary. They're all gone.

MARY: Not all of them. One bush didn't get crushed. A board protected it. And I picked the one rose that was still blooming. See, I kept it for you, Mr. Jones. *(Holds out a beautiful rose.)*

FRED: *(Faces audience.)* Thank you, Mary. Look, everyone. My prize rose. Just look at that.

GLADYS: It's beautiful, Fred.

FRED: *(Proudly.)* It's more than beautiful. It's perfect. Every petal just like velvet. See the color! And smell the perfume. *(They all sniff.)*

HARDING: It *is* perfect. God does a beautiful job with roses.

FRED: *(Stunned.)* What—what did you say?

HARDING: I said God does a beautiful job with roses. You couldn't make a rose, Fred. You can grow them but you can't make them.

FRED: No, I can't make them. *(Slowly.)* You know, I think I've been a fool. Someone greater than I am made roses and trees and air and everything on this earth. And he protected Jane and me, just the way he sheltered this one rose to bring me to my senses. Let me see—how does that song go?

> This is my Father's world.
> He shines in all that's fair.
> In the rustling grass I hear him pass.
> He speaks to me everywhere.

I think maybe God is beginning to speak to me through this rose.

JANE: Oh, Fred, I hope so.

FRED: Look, everyone. I can't understand why my house was blown down. Maybe someday I will. Maybe this all happened to show Jane and me what good friends we have. But I can't be angry at a God who made a rose. And a God who gave his son for me. I guess I'll have to trust him when it storms the way I do when the sun shines.

The Secret

Characters

DR. DALE TARRAT—Psychiatrist. Can be played by a woman if desired.

HENRY DARNEL—Town banker, impressed by own importance.

MISS JUNE MATTES—Timid, afraid, old maid type.

MRS. CARRIE LEXINGTON—Well educated, high strung.

MRS. PHYLLIS O'DAY—Spiritual figure, yet down to earth.

Setting

Plain stage. Three chairs in middle, a single chair on each side. A lectern can be used in center of stage but should not block the actors.

Costumes

Contemporary.

(As the scene opens, the five chairs on stage are vacant. A reading stand may also be used but should not block any of the chairs. DR. TARRAT enters from the left and advances to center stage.)

DR. TARRAT: Good evening, ladies and gentlemen. I am Doctor Dale Tarrat, psychiatrist. For the past twenty years I've been listening to hundreds of patients tell me their problems, their hopes and fears. If my files could be opened to the public, what a record of unhappiness and trouble *(Pause.)*, but of course that's impossible. All that my patients tell me is strictly confidential. But tonight I have a rare treat for you. Three individuals have agreed to share their stories with you and with one another. This is most unusual, so let me explain the circumstances. When I first meet a patient, I ask a simple question: If you could be someone different, who would you choose to be? I get some very revealing answers. Some want to be movie stars or famous politicians or athletic heroes. Such answers reveal hidden desires and ambitions and these guide me in my treatment.

Recently, three people named the same rather obscure woman as the person they most envied. The coincidence was too good to miss. So I have asked all three patients to tell you what they find so attractive about this one individual, Mrs. Phyllis O'Day. Unknown to them, I have also asked Mrs. O'Day to be present tonight. Perhaps through a few questions we can learn what these three people find so attractive about their idol and what is the real secret of Mrs. O'Day's life.

And now I must introduce my patients to you. *(Calling.)* Mr. Darnel, Miss Mattes, Mrs. Lexington, we're ready for you. *(They enter, greet DR. TARRAT and take the three seats center stage.)* I thank you all for coming this evening. I'm sure your stories will be helpful to everyone here. Mr. Darnel, suppose you begin by telling your problems to these nice people. (DARNEL *steps to center stage.* DR. TARRAT *sits on chair to right.*)

DARNEL: Thank you, Dr. Tarrat. My name is Henry Darnel and I am the town banker. I suppose I am the most important and influential man in this community. Over the past ten years my bank has tripled its deposits and I am the one responsible for that growth. I've worked hard to become a power here, and today, when any new project is proposed in this town, the first question every-one asks is, "What does Henry Darnel think of it?" If I approve, the project usually gets community support. Naturally I am pleased to have such influence. (*Change in tone.*) But I've paid a price for my progress and growth. My stomach has gone back on me, my nerves are on edge and I have to take too many tranquilizers in order to get a good night's sleep. And when I sleep, I have nightmares. (*Shudders.*) Real nightmares. Be-sides, I'm a stranger to my children and my wife is threatening to divorce me. That's why I became a patient of Dr. Tarrat.

DR. TARRAT: Thank you, Mr. Darnel. Now perhaps you will tell us why you are attracted to Mrs. O'Day.

DARNEL: (*Angry.*) I'm not attracted to her. Not in the usual sense of the word. But she comes into my bank every week, cashes the small paycheck she receives as Mrs. Lexington's maid and baby-sitter, and deposits a few dollars in her savings account. I know Mrs. O'Day doesn't have much money—at least she doesn't deposit much in my bank. And yet she has a radiance about her, a way of talking that makes everyone in the bank feel better. When she comes in, it's like the sun shining through the front windows and when she leaves it's as if the clouds have returned. Frankly, I don't know what she has to be so happy about. She seems to know a secret that makes her life different from most of my other customers. And I want to know what that secret is. I need her strength if I'm to continue making a success of my bank.

DR. TARRAT: Thank you, Mr. Darnel. (DARNEL *sits down.*) And now, Miss Mattes, please tell us about your problems.

MISS MATTES: *(Comes to center of stage, rather reluctantly.)* Yes, Doctor. I feel embarrassed in front of all these people but I promised to tell my story, so I might as well begin. My name is June Mattes. *Miss* June Mattes. I'm a single woman. Never got married—although I had some chances. I was afraid of marriage. So many couples end in the divorce court these days. I was afraid even to try. I guess I'm afraid of a lot of things. I know I worry about getting sick and about—dying. I've been to lots of doctors but none of them has been able to cure me. Some have even said there was nothing wrong with me and maybe they're right. Last year I thought I might help my troubles by talking to other people about their difficulties, so I volunteered to help the committee at my church, the one that calls on sick people. That's where I met Mrs. O'Day. She's on the committee too. She has the magic touch. Sometimes we call on people together and she cheers them up and I make them feel worse. Last month I went to see a sick woman and she told me not to come back again. Then they sent Mrs. O'Day and she was asked to come back as often as she could. I just can't understand it. She's a widow with three children to take care of. She has less money than I have and more problems. But she's always happy and I'm miserable. If only I could feel the way she does—*(Has been getting more emotional.)*

DR. TARRAT: *(Interrupting.)* That's enough, Miss Mattes. Don't get too worked up. Perhaps you'd better sit down now and let Mrs. Lexington speak.

MISS MATTES: Oh, yes. Thank you. *(She sits and* DR. TARRAT *nods to* MRS. LEXINGTON *who takes her place at stage center.)*

MRS. LEXINGTON: My name is Carrie Lexington. Mrs. Carrie Lexington. As you have already heard, Mrs. O'Day is my maid and baby-sitter. Please don't think I'm one of those rich women who sits around all day trying to look pretty. I go to work Monday through Friday and a good part of my salary goes to pay Mrs. O'Day for taking care of my family while I work. I don't like the arrangement but staying at home was what made me need to go to Dr. Tarrat for psychiatric help. I said Mrs. O'Day takes care of my family but I really only have a husband and one small boy, Timmy. Believe me, one small boy can be enough to drive you wild. I was going out of my mind with his crying and his questions and his demands for attention. And that's where Mrs. O'Day comes in. You see, I hired her to do the baby-sitting all day and to handle things around the house while I went to work. And it's turned out beautifully. Timmy seems entirely different when Mrs. O'Day is around. They get along so well. She tells him stories and listens to his silly questions. Even my husband sits and talks to my baby-sitter when he's home. I guess Mrs. O'Day is a good listener and I'm not. But there must be something else. How can she put up with everything—that bratty kid and my boring husband—and still be cheerful? There must be a secret to it and I want to know why she can be so calm and peaceful when I can hardly stand to be at home the two days a week that I don't work. *(Turning.)* Dr. Tarrat, you should have invited Mrs. O'Day here tonight. Then maybe we could all learn her secret.

DR. TARRAT: *(Bowing.)* How right you are, Mrs. Lexington. And that's just what I have done. Mrs. O'Day will be with us in a minute.

DARNEL: *(Jumping up.)* You mean you've got the woman right here?

MISS MATTES: Oh, I'll be afraid to look her in the face. What will she think of me, envying her?

MRS. LEXINGTON: You should have warned us, Doctor.

DR. TARRAT: Then you wouldn't have come. Tonight you can ask Mrs. O'Day any questions you want. She's promised to answer and to tell you all you want to know. *(Calling.)* Mrs. O'Day! Mrs. O'Day! Please come in.

MRS. O'DAY: *(Entering from opposite side of stage.)* Good evening, Dr. Tarrat. Good evening, everyone. *(They greet her. She sees audience.)* Oh, so many people.

DR. TARRAT: Please be seated, Mrs. O'Day. *(She sits at opposite end of stage from* DR. TARRAT.*)* As I explained to you, my three patients want to ask you some questions. They all have problems and perhaps you can help them.

MRS. O'DAY: I'm sure I don't know how. But I'll try.

DARNEL: This is most irregular but I don't suppose it can do any harm. Tell me, Mrs. O'Day, is my bank the only one where you deposit money?

MRS. O'DAY: Oh, yes. I don't have enough money to need two banks.

Darnel: Then you have other resources in stocks and bonds, perhaps? Or in real estate?

Mrs. O'Day: *(Laughs.)* You're making fun of me, Mr. Darnel. The savings account I have in your bank is all my "resources" as you call them.

Darnel: But that's unbelievable. Mrs. O'Day, suppose you were to get sick. Or one of your children were to have an accident? What would you do then?

Mrs. O'Day: The best I could.

Darnel: You'd have to borrow money.

Mrs. O'Day: Yes, and then I'd have to pay it back. But I never borrow trouble. I don't worry about what hasn't happened. So far I've had enough money to take care of my needs and to provide for my children's education. And if you have enough, you don't need any more.

Darnel: But—but—don't you want to get ahead?

Mrs. O'Day: Ahead of whom—or what? I'm happy the way I am.

Darnel: Oh, I give up. We don't talk the same language. *(Turns away.)*

Miss Mattes: I'm sure my friend Mrs. O'Day and I can talk the same language. We go to the same church and serve on the same committee.

Darnel: You talk to her then. She's beyond me.

Miss Mattes: I will. Tell me, Phyllis, have you been to see Mrs. Billings lately?

Mrs. O'Day: Yes, I was there last week.

Miss Mattes: Her relatives told me I shouldn't come again. Said I upset her. And we had such a nice talk, I thought, all about her ailments and mine. I enjoyed myself, but I guess that wasn't what she wanted. What did you do when you went? What did you say to her?

Mrs. O'Day: Nothing special. I told her we all loved her and were praying for her. Then I washed up her kitchen floor.

Miss Mattes: *(Astonished.)* Washed up her kitchen floor!

Mrs. O'Day: Yes, it was dirty.

Miss Mattes: I saw that. But how did you ever think to do such a thing?

Mrs. O'Day: I didn't have to think. I know how I like my floors. And Mrs. Billings couldn't do hers so I did it for her.

Miss Mattes: Didn't you talk about her sickness or anything like that?

Mrs. O'Day: I'm afraid not. We were too busy talking and laughing about other things.

Miss Mattes: Laughing yet. Well, I never.

Mrs. Lexington: Look, I've got to get into this. You two are just fooling around with trivial things. Mrs. O'Day, I want some straight answers. From the day you started working for me, you and my son have gotten along beautifully. Why?

Mrs. O'Day: Because he's a beautiful child.

Mrs. Lexington: Beautiful! He's a brat.

Mrs. O'Day: Yes, I suppose he is at times. Most children are. But Timmy just wants someone to listen to him. Life is big and wonderful when you're young. You need to share it with someone.

Mrs. Lexington: He's just a child!

Mrs. O'Day: Yes. So I become a child with him. We've explored every nook of your house and examined every blade of grass in your yard. It's wonderful, the secrets we've found there.

Mrs. Lexington: Are you saying I've been neglecting my child?

Mrs. O'Day: Of course not. Only, it helps to see life through a child's eyes. Maybe I don't have to stoop so much to enter a child's world. But Timmy and I have learned a lot about God and life and others.

Dr. Tarrat: I think I'm going to have to intervene here. Somehow we aren't getting at our real concerns. Mrs. O'Day, all three of my patients think you have some special way of living life and they want to know what it is.

Mrs. O'Day: I'm sure I don't know any secrets. I'm a Christian, if that's what you mean.

Miss Mattes: I'm a Christian too. But that doesn't solve my worries.

Mrs. Lexington: My husband and I go to church fairly regularly. Why should the church make things easier for you and not for me?

Darnel: I never miss a Sunday. A banker should attend church. It makes people feel safer about their money.

Dr. Tarrat: I'm afraid being a Christian isn't the whole answer, Mrs. O'Day. Most of the people I see in my office claim to be Christians. Yet they have lots of worries and troubles. Don't you have any more explanation than that?

Mrs. O'Day: Well—maybe it's my partner and my song that make the difference.

Miss Mattes: Your partner! I thought you were a widow.

Mrs. Lexington: Have you been hiding something from us?

Darnel: I knew there was more than meets the eye here.

Mrs. O'Day: Don't be foolish. I'm not talking about a human being. That is, not the kind you're thinking of. But you see, my husband died eight years ago and left me with three small children. Poor man, he worked hard to support us but he didn't leave me much money. So I knew I was in trouble.

Darnel: Spare us the hearts and flowers.

Mrs. O'Day: I'm not asking for sympathy. When I sat down to face my situation, I knew I couldn't do it alone. So I took the Lord in as my partner. I told him—I'll do the work but I can't work and worry at the same time. So, Lord, you take care of the worrying. And he has. I don't concern myself with problems, the kind Mr. Darnel was talking about a little while ago. When something comes up, I just say, Lord, that's your department. He's really a very good partner.

Miss Mattes: *(Almost crying.)* Oh, that sounds so nice. I wish I could think like that. But I'd be afraid even to try.

Darnel: Sounds like a lot of religious nonsense to me.

Mrs. Lexington: I'm going to have to give this more thought. But you said something about a song.

Mrs. O'Day: Oh, yes, my song. You see, years ago I learned a song in summer Bible school. And I've remembered that song and it's helped me through many a hard place.

Dr. Tarrat: Ah, the magic formula at last.

Mrs. O'Day: There's no magic about it. The song goes like this.

> O Master, let me walk with you
> In lowly paths of service true;
> Tell me your secret; help me bear
> The strain of toil, the fret of care.

I'm particularly fond of the third verse.

> Teach me your patience; share with me
> A closer, dearer company,
> In work that keeps faith sweet and strong,
> In trust that triumphs over wrong.

Somehow, when things get hard, that song gives me the help I need. I try to walk with Jesus every day. I want to do his work and be guided by what he wants me to do. That's why I can face every day, even though I don't have a large sum of money deposited in your bank, Mr. Darnel. And that's why I can wash up Mrs. Billings' floor and can get along with Timmy, Mrs. Lexington. I simply try to do what I think God wants me to do.

Darnel: And you don't have any worries or problems?

Mrs. O'Day: Of course I do. Nobody can keep from having problems on their doorstep in this world. But I don't rent out space in my heart for worries. I pass them on to the Master who lets me walk with him.

Mrs. Lexington: And that's all you can tell us? That's the secret that made us envy you?

Mrs. O'Day: That's the way I live, but there's no secret about it. Everybody can live that way.

Darnel: *(Standing up.)* I think I've been cheated. I thought I was going to learn some great solution to my problems tonight. But this—this is just not my style. Excuse me. *(Exits.)*

MRS. LEXINGTON: It's not my style either. I couldn't operate with such a simple solution to life's complexities. Walk with the Master! Make the Lord your partner! Well, really—(*Exits.*)

MISS MATTES: I guess I'm the only one left. And I do like what you said, Phyllis. I'm so glad it works for you. But I have so many problems. I'm afraid—afraid it won't do for me. (*Exits.*)

MRS. O'DAY: They're all gone, Dr. Tarrat. I guess I haven't been much help. Can I go now?

DR. TARRAT: Yes, you may go. And thank you for coming, Mrs. O'Day. (*She exits. He moves to stage center and talks to audience.*) You've heard three fools and one wise woman tonight. Mrs. O'Day knows the answer to worries and anxieties. But those three patients of mine couldn't recognize the truth when they heard it. Too bad. (*Pause.*) Still, if it weren't for fools like those three, I wouldn't have any patients to counsel. (*He exits.*)

A History Lesson

Characters

All the characters are teen-agers of high school or college age.

JAMES—A bit studious.

BARBARA—Religious, hard-working student.

NORMAN—Lively, cynical at times.

SUE—Careful, hard worker.

CANDACE—A little scatterbrained.

Setting

Living room at BARBARA's home. A small table where JAMES and BARBARA are studying. Table piled with books. Three other chairs in room. Other furnishings as desired. A hymnal lying on a table someplace.

Costumes

Ordinary teen-age dress.

(As the scene opens, JAMES *and* BARBARA *are seated at a small table, studying. There is a knock at the door.* JAMES *stands up.)*

JAMES: I'll get it.

BARBARA: All right. But tell whoever's there we're busy. We've got to get this assignment done.

JAMES: OK. *(Opens the door.)* Oh, it's the gang—Candace, Norman, and Sue. The gruesome threesome.

NORMAN: *(Steps in.)* That's us, in person. We were thrown out of the library for making too much noise so we thought we'd come over here for a while until you throw us out too. Can we come in?

BARBARA: *(Standing up.)* Oh, all right. *(They all enter and nod to one another.)* But James and I are busy. He came over a little while ago and we've been hitting the books ever since. Sit down, everyone. *(They all sit or sprawl.)*

SUE: We were busy too, working on that world history assignment. Only we got to laughing at Candace and the librarian told us to take our business someplace else.

JAMES: We've been wrestling with the same project. Seems kinda tough to come up with something.

CANDACE: The whole assignment is a bummer. Old man Winker must be out of his gourd. *(Reads from notebook.)* Imagine you were a newspaper reporter living during one of the crises we have been studying in this class. Write some headlines, recording the news of that day. *(Looks up.)* Isn't that weird!

BARBARA: I don't know. I thought it was a kinda clever project. Better than memorizing a lot of dates. Or taking one of those stupid true-false tests where the smartest guesser gets the best grade.

CANDACE: Yeah, I suppose you're right. Anyway, I've got my headlines done, so I don't have to worry.

NORMAN: You should hear those headlines. Laughing at them was what got us thrown out of the library. When old Winker reads them, he'll probably have a heart attack and we'll never be able to complete the course.

CANDACE: Oh, don't be so silly, Norman.

BARBARA: You've got my curiosity ready to boil over. What crisis did you pick, Candace?

CANDACE: The Americans at Valley Forge. We studied that last week, so I figured I would remember it best.

JAMES: *(Sneering.)* Half the class will pick Valley Forge.

SUE: But they won't have Candace's dizzy headlines. Wait until you hear them.

JAMES: Well, for goodness sake, read them, Candace.

CANDACE: All right. I got to thinking about the lonely days at Valley Forge and how hopeless the American cause must have seemed to lots of the soldiers. So this is what I wrote. *(She reads the headlines from a paper or from a poster she has with her.)*

"WE'LL BEAT 'EM YET," SAYS GEORGIE W.

NEW RECRUIT CONFESSES:
"I'VE GOT COLD FEET"

"BRITISH WILL WIN BY SPRING,"
PREDICTS CORNWALLIS

NORMAN: Isn't that a gasser? I'll bet that's the first time anybody ever called General Washington "Georgie W." He wasn't a guy you could kid around with.

CANDACE: Oh, he wasn't so stiff. It's just his wooden teeth

that make him look forbidding. I'll bet his wife Martha called him Georgie—among other things.

JAMES: I like the part about the soldier with cold feet. It really fills me with patriotic fervor.

CANDICE: You can all poke fun but I'm handing this assignment in, just the way I read it.

BARBARA: I don't think Valley Forge was very funny. The history of this country and of the whole world would have been different if Washington hadn't found strength to go on with the struggle. Maybe we wouldn't have freedom of religion or any other freedom if our ancestors hadn't survived that crisis.

NORMAN: You really make it sound important. But how about hearing my headlines now. I didn't pick out anything so obvious as Valley Forge. I went back to the first century A.D. to the time when Rome burned while Nero fiddled and then accused the Christians of starting the whole mess.

BARBARA: That sounds interesting. I wouldn't have minded living back then. If I could have stayed out of Nero's way.

NORMAN: With your religious beliefs you wouldn't have stood a chance. But did you ever stop to think if Nero had had his way, there wouldn't be any Christianity today. Not that I care, of course. But somehow the Christians won and survived the crisis. Seems hard to believe, but they had something back then that was tougher than Nero and the whole Roman empire.

JAMES: Since you don't have much use for religion, why did you pick that crisis for your report?

NORMAN: Because I liked the way Winker described the whole situation. It was almost as if he had been there.

SUE: As one of the lions, ready to eat a Christian, no doubt.

NORMAN: OK. Hold your breath. Here come my headlines. *(Reads like a newsboy from notebook or poster as before.)* Extra, extra! Read all about it.
"CHRISTIANS ARE ARSONISTS AND ATHEISTS," SAYS NERO
"I'LL MAKE IT HOT FOR EVERY CHRISTIAN IN THE EMPIRE"
EMPEROR'S FIDDLE ESCAPES FIRE—UNFORTUNATELY
That ought to make Winker sit up and take notice. Especially if he lets me read my report out loud.

BARBARA: Out loud, he says. You'll burst people's eardrums two blocks away.

JAMES: You two seem to be in good shape. How about you, Sue?

SUE: Well—I think I've got mine done. I decided to use a real romantic crisis in history.

NORMAN: She's been watching too many soap operas.

SUE: There were some romantic occurrences in history even before TV put its oar in. I picked the Battle of Actium, between the forces of Anthony and Cleopatra and those of Octavius Caesar. It was fought in 31 B.C.

NORMAN: Wow! That happened before I was born.

JAMES: That's the trouble with history. Most of it happened so long ago. Makes it hard to remember.

CANDACE: Will you two comedians keep quiet and let Sue read her headlines! She's got some beautiful ones.

JAMES: OK. Fire away.

SUE: Just in case you C students don't remember, let me remind you that the Battle of Actium gave world supremacy to the West, rather than to Egypt and the Middle East. But the battle was all mixed up with Anthony's love for Cleopatra and his deserting his wife for the Egyptian siren. So my headlines aren't funny. They're more like the kinds of things you read in those papers they sell at supermarkets. Here they are. *(Reads as before.)*

LOVERS RISK THE WORLD FOR LOVE

THE ETERNAL TRIANGLE, ON LAND AND SEA

MARK ANTHONY: CLEOPATRA'S SLAVE
OR OCTAVIUS' SLAVE?

CANDACE: That sounds like something out of Hollywood. It should make Winker's heart beat faster, if he's got a heart.

NORMAN: Might know a girl would pick a silly crisis like that.

BARBARA: Don't you sell Actium short. It meant a lot to Christians, even though it happened before Jesus was born. With Rome in charge of the civilized world it was easier for those first apostles to spread the good news of the gospel throughout the empire. It might have been different if Cleopatra had won.

NORMAN: Might know you'd give a religious twist to the whole story. I just wish I'd have lived back then so I could have gotten a glimpse of that Egyptian queen.

CANDACE: You probably would have been disappointed. I'll bet she was fat and wore too much rouge.

NORMAN: Somebody always pouring cold water on my dreams.

Sᴜᴇ: Say, Barbara, you and James haven't shown us your headlines. What have you come up with?

Bᴀʀʙᴀʀᴀ: I'm afraid we haven't gotten anything written down yet. We'd just decided on our historical events when you knocked at the door.

Sᴜᴇ: Well, James, did you pick Valley Forge too? Is that why you sneered at Candace?

Jᴀᴍᴇs: Nothing cheap like that. I've chosen the Battle of Tours in 732 when Charles the Hammerer defeated the Mohammedans and stopped their advance into Europe. If that hadn't happened, we might be praying to Allah. And the men might be marrying four wives.

Cᴀɴᴅᴀᴄᴇ: Hurrah for Charles—I think.

Jᴀᴍᴇs: It was a real crisis and a great victory. Christianity was on the spot again. Seems like the church is always in trouble and yet always muddles through at the last minute.

Nᴏʀᴍᴀɴ: You're choking me with all this religion. But get those headlines done. And Barbara, what titillating crisis have you chosen? I'm almost afraid to ask.

Bᴀʀʙᴀʀᴀ: You're not going to like my choice, I know. But I got tired of thinking about battles and slaughter and bloodshed. So I picked the appearance of Martin Luther at the Diet of Worms. That began the Protestant movement in Europe. And all modern history dates from the breakup of the medieval church.

Nᴏʀᴍᴀɴ: I might have known. You're always talking about religion. But do you know whether Winker is a Protestant or a Roman Catholic? It might make a difference in your grades.

BARBARA: I doubt that he's concerned about religion at all. But he did say in class that the Reformation was good for both sides. Made everybody keep on their toes. So maybe my grade will be safe, if that really matters. But I still haven't thought up any snappy headlines.

NORMAN: How about MONK MAKES MONKEY OUT OF THE EMPEROR? I'll give you that one free.

BARBARA: Your generosity is overwhelming.

SUE: I think we should go now and let you two work on your projects. Glad we've got ours done.

JAMES: But you haven't. Don t you remember the rest of the assignment? You're supposed to write a paragraph or two explaining why the crisis turned out the way it did.

CANDACE: We are? *(Leafs through notes.)* Yes, you're right. I've got that written down in my notes.

NORMAN: Why didn't you tell us? You know Sue and I missed that day in class.

CANDACE: I just forgot. Anyway, it won't be too hard for me. Valley Forge is easy to explain.

SUE: How do you figure that?

CANDACE: Well, it was the good guys versus the bad guys. The Americans were supposed to win because they were right. And the British were bound to lose because they were on the wrong side. It's as simple as that.

NORMAN: Oh, boy! White hats versus black hats. That's some theory of history. Don't you remember, my little scatterbrain, that old Winker said there were good people on both sides and that some of the people in Washington's army were just trying to get out of paying debts to the Tories?

CANDACE: I heard him say that but I didn't believe it. But if you're so smart, how are you going to explain why Nero didn't get rid of all the Christians, even though he threatened to do it. What's your theory of history?

NORMAN: I don't have any. I don't think you can explain anything. History just happens. It's all blind chance. Another time Nero might have won and the Christians have been wiped out.

SUE: That won't convince Winker. You'll need more explanation than that!

NORMAN: All right. What are you going to say about your little crisis? Did Anthony and Cleopatra lose because they were immoral and Octavius was faithful to his wife? You'll sound like Candace if you offer that explanation.

SUE: I think I know better than to offer such a flimsy excuse. Battles are won by smart people, not moral or immoral people. It's brains that make the difference in this world and Octavius was smarter than his two opponents. He used lighter ships and managed to set fires on the enemy boats. It's as simple as that. Brains always win in the end.

NORMAN: It's easy to say that after everything is over. The one who wins is the smart one. You can't lose with that explanation.

JAMES: I think Sue is right. But you've got to add something else to what she said. History is always written by the winners. Take the battle I chose. We in the West think it was a victory. Mohammedan historians have a different viewpoint. It all depends on who is doing the telling.

NORMAN: That makes sense to me.

SUE: I agree. The winner always has the last word.

BARBARA: I'm sorry but I don't agree with any of you. You've got too glib an explanation.

NORMAN: Well now, Miss Socrates, suppose you slip us the real dope on everything.

BARBARA: I think you are all leaving the Lord out of the picture.

NORMAN: I might have known. We're going to get a sermon.

BARBARA: No sermon. But I refuse to believe the world passes through all kinds of crises like the ones we've been discussing and yet God completely ignores what's happening.

NORMAN: *(Sneering.)* Maybe he's busy elsewhere. Maybe that's why we have crises. Nobody's watching the store and things get into a mess.

BARBARA: You can scoff if you want to. And I know Winker never mentioned God in all his lectures. But I believe God made this world and placed human beings on it. And he isn't the kind of God to start something and then neglect it.

JAMES: You mean you think God takes a hand every time there's trouble? That he sees to it that the right side wins? Aren't you just taking Candace's white hats versus black hats explanation and making it a little fancier by adding God to the mixture?

BARBARA: I don't think I am. And I can't tell you why the British lost the Revolutionary War or why Octavius Caesar defeated Anthony and Cleopatra. I only know God doesn't desert his world. James, get me that hymnal over there on the table. *(He reaches it and hands it to her.)*

CANDACE: Are you going to sing for us?

BARBARA: No, I'll spare you that. But there's a hymn in here that says clearly what I'm struggling to say. *(Leafs through book.)* Oh, yes, here it is. Now listen. *(Reads hymn, verses 1, 2.)*

> O God, our help in ages past,
> Our hope for years to come,
> Our shelter from the stormy blast,
> And our eternal home:
> Under the shadow of your throne
> Your saints have dwelt secure;
> Sufficient is your arm alone,
> And our defence is sure.

SUE: That does sound pretty good.

NORMAN: Sure it sounds good. But it hasn't always worked out that way. What about the times when Christians were persecuted and no one came to their rescue? What about Christians behind the iron curtain today? Seems to me it's better to say things just happen and let it go at that.

BARBARA: I understand what you're saying. But listen to the fourth verse of this hymn.

> A thousand ages in your sight
> Are like an evening gone,
> Short as the watch that ends the night
> Before the rising sun.

You can't make God fit our timetable. You can't tell him how to run the world. If I've learned anything in that history class, I've learned that almost unbelievable events do occur. But you have to trust in God and believe he will eventually make all things right.

NORMAN: How? How?

BARBARA: I don't know. That's where faith comes in. You've

got to believe in him, believe God is in charge of his world. He didn't desert his Son in the grave. And he won't desert us.

Sue: Old Winker will never buy that explanation. I'm sure he won't.

Barbara: You're probably right. But I'm going to put it in my report anyway.

Candace: Do you think you should? Winker will probably just laugh at you.

Barbara: The truth has been laughed at before. Maybe Winker isn't too old to learn that history is more than dates and crises and explanations. Maybe we all need to learn there's someone behind the scenes, someone who has never forgotten his people and won't forget us today.